My Friend, Jesus

Pictures by
Ferelith Eccles Williams

Collins

At school
I make new friends.
We have secrets,
  and make plans,
  and do all sorts of things together.
Sometimes, one of my friends
  comes to my home,
  or we go out together.

For me to do
I will write a story, or draw a picture,
about when one of my friends
came to my home.
I will put in it
some of the special things we do together.

A prayer to pray
Loving Father,
I like my friends.
We talk and play,
we share our secrets,
we watch television together.
It's good to have a friend.

Father, your love gives us friends.
Thank you.

I make new friends at school

Jesus had many friends.
This is a story about three of them.

There were two sisters, Martha and Mary,
and they had a brother called Lazarus.
They lived together in a house in Bethany.
Jesus was their friend.
One day he came to visit them.

Martha was very busy getting a meal ready,
setting everything out neat and tidy,
finding special things to eat and drink,
to welcome her friend, Jesus.

Mary just sat there, talking with Jesus,
    listening to him,
    looking at him.
She just wanted to be with him
all the time she could.

A prayer to pray
Lord Jesus, you are my friend.
Sometimes I am cheerful and busy,
and have lots of things to do.
Be with me then.

Sometimes I'm quiet,
sometimes I'm lonely,
sometimes I just want to sit and think.
Be with me then.

Jesus had many friends

Jesus and his friends had been walking
for a long time.
They were hot and dusty, tired and hungry.
While the others went to get food
Jesus sat down to rest, beside a water well.
A woman came along to draw some water.
She was a Samaritan.

Most Jews would not have spoken to her,
because she was a woman,
and because they despised Samaritans.
But Jesus was a very friendly person,
and he asked her to give him a drink,
and had a long chat with her.

She liked him so much
that she ran back to her village
to bring her friends out to meet him, too.

For me to do
Are there people at school
    that nobody plays with?
Do I know anyone who hasn't any friends?
I will ask them to join in our game tomorrow.
I will try to make friends with them.

A prayer to pray
Lord Jesus,
you were friendly to everyone you met.
Help me to be like you.

Jesus was a very friendly person

There was a man called Zaccheus.
Nobody liked him much,
because he was a tax collector.
Zaccheus wanted to see Jesus for himself.
One day he heard that Jesus was coming.
He climbed up into a tree
so he could see over the heads of the crowd.
Jesus stopped. He looked up and called out:
'Zaccheus, come down.
Today I want to have dinner at your house.'

What a celebration they had—
Zaccheus got out his best to eat and drink,
and they had a great time.
And now that Jesus was his friend,
Zaccheus wanted to be good. He promised
to pay back anyone he had cheated,
and to give half his money to the poor.

For me to do
Zaccheus had to try hard to get to know Jesus:
 I will write down four things
 that Zaccheus does in the story.
What can I do to get to know Jesus?
 I will write down two things I can do.

A prayer to pray
Lord Jesus, come to me and be my friend,
just like you did to Zaccheus.
I will try to show I love you by what I do.

8

Jesus makes friends with a tax collector

My Dad likes to make things.
He cuts the wood to the right length,
smooths it with the plane,
drills the wall, plugs it,
and fixes the shelf, strong and neat.
I help if I can. I like working with Dad.

My friend and I make things together.
We built some model houses,
and now we can make up games
to play with them.

For me to do
I will look out for ways to help
   with the work at home.
I will make a plan with my friend
for something special we can do together.

A prayer to pray
Lord God,
the world is full of interesting things to do.
Make my arms strong,
make my fingers nimble,
make me see straight,
so I can do good work.

Lord,
I like doing things with my friends.
Thank you for the good times we have together.

Friends work together

Jesus worked with his friends

Several of Jesus' friends were fishermen.
Jesus sometimes went fishing with them.
One night, they set off without him.
They fished all night long,
but they caught nothing at all.
When morning came,
they were tired and disappointed.
They rowed back to the shore
and there they saw Jesus.
'Throw out your nets again', he called.
'What's the use', said Peter.
'We've caught nothing all night.'

But they did as Jesus said,
and so many fish were caught in the net
that they could hardly pull it in.
Meanwhile,
Jesus had picked up wood from the beach.
He made a fire
and cooked some fish for their breakfast.

A prayer to pray
Lord Jesus,
help me with my work.
I often find it difficult.
I get tired and fed up
when I can't get it to go right.
Help me to keep on trying.

Jesus said to his friends: 'Go out,
and tell everyone the Good News about me.
Tell everyone
that God sent me into the world to do his work:
• to let everyone know that God loves them
• to make sick people well
• to set people free from sorrow and suffering
• to bring all men and women into God's family.
I will always be with you,
and I will help you when you do my work.'

Jesus kept his promise
and that is how I know about him today.
The Good News about Jesus
was told to me by his friends —
• by my mother and father
• by my teachers
• by people in the church.

For me to think about
Now it is my turn to help Jesus with his work.

A prayer to pray
Lord Jesus,
you are my friend.
Help me to let other people see your goodness:
    by the things I do
    by the sort of person I am.
Help me to love and serve you, Lord Jesus.

Jesus gives his friends work to do

Jesus helps his friends

Jesus was teaching in the streets of a city.
A Roman officer came to him and said:
'Sir, my servant is sick.'
Jesus said: 'I will come home with you
and make him better.'
The officer said: 'Oh, no, Lord.
I am not worthy for you
to come into my house.
Just you say the word, you give the order,
and my servant will get better.'
So that's what Jesus did.
'Go home', he said to the officer,
'and because you believe in my power,
your servant will be well again.'

For me to think about
Jesus was always doing things for people:
• he helped the Roman officer
• he went home with Zaccheus and made friends
• he visited his friends Martha and Mary

I will write a story or draw a picture
about one thing Jesus has done for me.

A prayer to pray
Lord Jesus,
help those who are sick in my town,
help those who are lonely or sad.
Help me to be a good friend to my friends.

Jesus said: 'When I come again, as King,
I shall say to my friends:
"Come, you blessed ones,
come into the kingdom that is ready for you.
When I was hungry, you gave me food.
When I was thirsty, you gave me a drink.
When I was a stranger, you took me home.
When I had no clothes, you gave me clothes.
When I was sick, you looked after me.
When I was in prison, you came to visit me."
My friends will ask: "Lord, when did we do this?"
And I will say: "Whatever you did for others,
however unimportant they were, you did for me."'

For me to think about
When I make a cup of coffee for my father,
when I help my mother carry the shopping,
when I keep the baby happy by playing with him,
when I talk to the old lady up the street—
I am doing these things for Jesus, my friend.

What else can I do for Jesus?
    I will ask my friends to help me,
    and we will work out a plan
    to do something special to help other people.

A prayer to pray
Lord, you care about everyone.
Help me to love others because you love them.

Jesus tells how he will know his friends

Jesus was preaching to the crowds.
He said 'I am the bread of life.
If anyone eats this bread,
he will live for ever.'
Many people in the crowd said:
'What nonsense is he talking?
We know this man.
He is the son of Joseph, isn't he?
How can he give us the bread of life?'
They got very angry, and many walked away
and wouldn't listen to Jesus any more.

Then Jesus said to his friends, the disciples:
'Are you going to leave me too?'
But Peter said: 'Lord, who would we go to?
You tell us the truth.
We know you are the holy one from God.'

For me to think about
It is not always easy to follow Jesus.
How can I stay close to Jesus?
• I can pray, and ask him to help me.
• I can read about Jesus, and get to know him.
• I can try to work out what is right
  and what is wrong, and to do what is right.

A prayer to pray
Lord, help me to know you more clearly,
to love you more dearly,
and to follow you more nearly.

Jesus' friends do not desert him

After Jesus died and was buried, his friends were very sad. Two of them were walking on the road to Emmaus, when Jesus came up and joined them, but they did not recognize him. He asked them what they were talking about.

'Haven't you heard about Jesus of Nazareth?' they said. 'We thought he was the Saviour, but now he's been killed and we don't know what to do.'

As they walked along the road, the stranger explained to them the meaning of his suffering and death. When they came home, they asked him in to eat with them. At the table he took a piece of bread and broke it—and then they realized that it was Jesus.

He disappeared from their sight. But they jumped up, full of joy, and ran all the way back to Jerusalem to tell the others what they had seen.

For me to think about
Often I feel very sad and gloomy
and it seems useless to keep on trying.
I will remember that
Jesus is always here with me,
even when I do not recognize him.

A prayer to pray
Lord Jesus, help me to recognize you
in the strangers I pass by in the street,
and in the people I live with every day.
Help me to know that you are always with me.

Jesus comforts his friends when they are sad

At Christmas and Easter
we have a celebration.
Lovely things to eat and drink, and lots of it.

On my birthday, I may have a special cake,
and perhaps a party.

Our friends and our family come
to share the celebrations.
We sing songs:
    Christmas carols, and 'Happy Birthday'.
We give gifts to the people who come.
We share the party food and have a good time.

For me to do
I will find out about the times
when Jesus ate with his friends.
I know about when he ate with Martha and Mary,
and with Zaccheus,
and when he cooked fish for breakfast
on the beach with his friends.
    I will try to find out about other times
    when Jesus ate with his friends.

A prayer to pray
Father in heaven, when we have a party
with good food and drink, we are happy.
We like being with each other and celebrating.
Your love gives us all these good things.
Thank you.

We have parties with our friends

Jesus shares a special meal with his friends

Jesus said to his friends:
'Go and get a room ready.
I want to eat a special meal with you
before I suffer and die.'

He sat at the table
with his twelve friends.
While they were eating,
Jesus took some bread
and said a prayer of thanks.
He broke the bread,
gave it to his disciples, and said:
'Take this and eat it.
This is my body.'

When supper was over,
Jesus took a cup of wine.
He gave thanks to God,
gave the cup to his disciples, and said:
'Take this and drink from it.
This is the cup of my blood.
Do this to remember me.'

For me to think about
Jesus gave himself to his friends.
He gives himself to us, too,
so that we will become more like him.

A prayer to pray
Let us give thanks to the Lord
for all that he is doing for us.

When we go to church we celebrate.
All of us who belong to God's family
—our friends, our neighbours, our relations,
people who are strangers to us—
all come together in the church.

We sing to praise God and his Son Jesus.

We give gifts—
bread and wine are taken to the altar;
we give money that we have earned by our work.
We give ourselves
—our own life and happiness and sorrow.

We take part in the meal of God's family
in holy communion,
when Jesus gives himself to all his family.

For me to do
Next time I go to church
I will notice how we celebrate:
- when do we sing?
- when do we give our gifts to God?
- when does Jesus give himself to us?

A prayer to pray
Our Father,
in your church I join with all your family
to offer you prayer and praise.
Lord, we are glad to be together
and to know that you are with us.

At church, all Jesus' friends are happy together

The whole world is invited to God's party

Jesus told this story
to show that God is the friend of everyone.
'There was once a king
who was going to hold a great feast for his son.
He sent his servants out
to invite all his friends to the party.
But they would not come.
One said: 'I have just bought an ox,
    and I must try it out.'
Another said: 'I have just got married.
    I can't leave my wife.'

So the king said to his servant:
'Forget about them.

Go out into the highways and byways
and invite everyone you meet to my feast.
Bring in the poor, the crippled, the blind—
get them all to come.' And they did.
So the king held his feast—
everyone who wanted to come was welcome.

A prayer to pray
Lord God our Father, every day you invite me
to share in all the good things you have made.
You invited me to join your special family
when I was baptised.
You invite me, when this life is over,
to be part of your family in heaven.

I will say 'Yes' to all your invitations.

Dear Parents,
Jesus was a real man. He liked people; he made friends;
he enjoyed doing things with his friends. Help your child
to get to know Jesus, who offers his friendship to each
one of us. His friendship opens up to us the boundless
love of God our Father. Read the stories in this book, talk
about the pictures, pray the prayers and make up others
of your own together. Talk over what happens each day
in your child's life and friendships, and seek out together
God's love for you in these things.

Collins Liturgical Publications
187 Piccadilly, London W1V 9DA

ISBN 0 00 599643 0
© text and illustrations 1980, William Collins Sons & Co Ltd
First published 1980

Made and printed in Great Britain
by William Collins Sons & Co Ltd, Glasgow